PATIOS, POTS
&
WINDOW BOXES

SUE AND ROGER NORMAN

Illustrations by
ELAINE FRANKS

This edition first published in 1997 by
Parragon
Units 13–17 Avonbridge Trading Estate
Atlantic Road, Avonmouth
Bristol BS11 9QD

Produced by
Robert Ditchfield Publishers

ISBN 0 75252 145 4

A copy of the British Library Cataloguing in Publication
Data is available from the Library.

Typeset by Action Typesetting Ltd, Gloucester
Colour origination by Colour Quest Graphic Services Ltd,
London E9
Printed and bound in Italy

"With thanks to J"

SYMBOLS

Where measurements are given, the first is the plant's height
followed by its spread.
The following symbols are also used in this book:
 ○ = thrives best or only in full sun
 ◑ = thrives best or only in part-shade
 ● = succeeds in full shade
 E = evergreen
Where no sun symbol and no reference to sun or shade is
made in the text, it can be assumed that the plant tolerates
sun or light shade.

POISONOUS PLANTS

Many plants are poisonous and it must be assumed that no
part of a plant should be eaten unless it is known that it is
edible.

CONTENTS

PATIOS, POTS AND WINDOW BOXES

A patio or paved area next to your house can be a joy for ever, if you get it right. The site will usually dictate the materials to be used and plants that will grow best.

Away from the house, paved or terraced areas give much more freedom in the choice of plants and construction materials.

Think carefully how you want to use the area. If you want a barbecue, then more of your patio will need to provide a level, uncluttered space for tables and chairs. If it is to be used by children, then safe surfaces and few vulnerable pots will be required. If plants are to be the main interest, then the aspect of the site will dictate what will grow best.

You must consider your planting plans at the design stage. The range of choices is enormous. Crevice planting? Borders? Raised beds? Pots and containers? Water feature? Climbers?

Be careful to choose materials which blend or contrast effectively with the surroundings and which are practical. Do not use gravel where children run, or where it will be walked into the house, and beware of smooth surfaces in shaded areas; they can be very slippery in winter.

Be sure to use adequate foundations and that the area drains properly.

PLANTING PATIOS AND TERRACES

How you plant your paved area will depend a lot on how much time you have available to look after it. It is no use developing a mass planting scheme in pots

Opposite: This patio has room to sit beneath a pergola.

A flight of steps shows off potted plants to advantage.

and containers for summer colour on a hot patio if you are not going to be there to water it twice a day in high summer, although there are automatic watering systems which would help.

Planting in containers has the enormous advantage of flexibility. You can have different schemes throughout the year and can grow plants that would not grow in your garden soil.

Beds offer easier growing conditions – larger root runs and less demanding watering – but are less flexible. Raised beds offer the added dimension of height and can be filled with the soil of your choice.

Many plants like to grow in the gaps between paving. This environment gives a cool root run which does not dry out quickly and, if the gaps are filled with gravel, this ensures a dry area round the

A row of trimmed box in pots gives the effect of a neat hedge.

neck of the plant, which is much appreciated by many alpines. Areas which are heavily walked on require tougher, shorter plants.

PLANTING

Almost any plant can be grown in a container: even forest trees can be grown as Bonsai subjects. It is important to strike the right balance between size of plant, size of pot, compost strength and plant vigour. It is better to repot a plant frequently than to put a small plant straight into a large container.

Loam-based composts are the easiest to use for plants in pots and containers; they hold moisture and fertilizers better than other composts. Possible exceptions to this are composts for hanging baskets

A tiny terrace with scented lilies beside the seat.

and window boxes, where weight is an important consideration.

It is necessary to use an ericaceous compost for rhododendrons, azaleas, heathers and other lime-hating plants.

Most plants need feeding and this can be achieved by adding fertilizers to the compost and by liquid feeding when watering. Annuals and soft perennials planted closely to flower over a long period need a strong compost and frequent liquid feeds. Trees and shrubs need a compost with relatively large amounts of slow release fertilizer, liquid feeding and annual repotting. They can be maintained in their final containers for some years by removing annually in spring as much compost as

A lovely and slightly tender *Abutilon megapotamicum*.

possible, without too much root disturbance, and replacing with fresh compost containing controlled-release fertilizer. Trees and shrubs will also need pruning to give them shape and to improve flowering.

Plants in containers tend to dry out very quickly and need frequent watering. During hot summer periods, hanging baskets and some pots will need watering twice a day. Equipment can be used to help with watering. Additives are also available which are designed to retain water in the compost and to aid rewetting dried-out composts.

Most annuals and soft perennials need dead-heading regularly to keep them flowering throughout the season.

1. PLANTING A PATIO

PAVING PLANTS

PLANTS IN THE GAPS BETWEEN PAVING soften the edges and add interest to your patio. Take care to leave clear walking areas. Thymes, creeping mints and chamomile may be planted on the edges of routes, as they tolerate bruising and are aromatic, whereas sempervivums are easily broken and do better in a sunny corner, out of the way of people's feet.

There are many varieties of **sempervivum (houseleeks)**, all of them decorative, even heraldic in shape with their evergreen rosettes and starry flowers in summer. After flowering, the individual rosette dies, but surrounding offsets continue. ○, E, 10cm/4in by indefinite spread.

Scilla sibirica Easy spring bulb, blooming year after year, needing little attention.
◐ 10–15cm/4–6in tall

Campanula cochleariifolia var. ***pallida* 'Miranda'** One of the very best with many slate-blue flowers.
5 × 60cm/2in × 2ft

Troughs combine well with paved areas, adding height and more planting opportunities. Pots, or ornaments, can be used to emphasize pathways and to lead the eye to the rest of the garden.

◆ *Almost fill the crevice with gravel round the neck of the plant, to conserve moisture and ease weeding.*

Erinus alpinus (**Fairy foxglove**) For walls and crevices. Flowers are various pinks and white.
○, E, 2.5–5cm/1–2in tall

Phlox subulata Evergreen mat. Spring-flowering. Many different forms, any colour except yellow. ○, E, 10 × 30–60cm/4in × 1–2ft

***Acaena* 'Blue Haze'** Spreading mats of steel-blue leaflets and sticky dark red burr heads in summer.
E, 10 × 60cm/4in × 2ft

Cotoneaster congestus Small white flowers in spring, large red berries.
E, mat-forming

***Trifolium repens* 'Purpurascens'** Purple-leaved form of the common clover. ○, mat-forming

Ajuga reptans There are many forms with different coloured leaves.
15 × 45cm/6in × 1½ft

EVERGREENS
and SMALL TREES

EVERGREENS AND SMALL TREES provide a long term shape to a patio, giving a quiet background to spring, summer colour and some interest in the winter. They are fairly permanent features and should be chosen with care.

Magnolia stellata One of the best dwarf shrubby trees. Flowers, white, scented, mid-spring.
2.4 × 2.4m/8 × 8ft

Thuja occidentalis **'Rheingold'** Conifers come in many different forms and shapes.
E, 1m × 60cm/3 × 2ft

Buxus sempervirens **(Box)** This tough evergreen shrub can be used for topiary and has many variegated forms.
E, 2.7 × 2.7m/9 × 9ft

◆ *Here the box has been trimmed to form balls in tubs.*

***Choisya ternata* (Mexican orange blossom)** Appreciates a
sheltered sunny position. Flowers, white, mainly in spring.
The glossy leaves are aromatic when crushed.
E, 2 × 2.4m/6 × 8ft

◆ *'Aztec Pearl' and 'Sundance' are attractive varieties of choisya.*

Artemisia 'Powis Castle'
Aromatic silver filigree
foliage contrasts with bright
summer colours.
E, 60 × 60cm/2 × 2ft

Hypericum olympicum
Small shrub with grey-green
leaves and golden yellow
flowers in summer.
◯, 30 × 30cm/1 × 1ft

Laurus nobilis (Sweet bay)
Often trimmed to make a
topiary ball. Needs shelter.
◯, E, 6 × 6m/20 × 20ft

**_Lonicera nitida_ 'Baggesen's
Gold'** Small-leaved
evergreen. Keeps its colour
well in winter.
◯, 1.5 × 2m/5 × 6ft

Erica arborea alpina
Compact tree heath with
plumes of tiny white flower
bells in winter/spring. E,
1.2m/4ft height and spread

Camellia **'Frau Minna Seidel'** ('Otome' 'Pink Perfection') Early flowers. Shelter from early morning sun.
◑, E, 2 × 2m/6 × 6ft

Cistus **'Elma'** Papery flowers open in the morning and fall in the evening, more appearing each day in summer.
○, E, 1.2 × 1.2m/4 × 4ft

Daphne tangutica Slow growing, easy. Flowers in early summer. Red berries.
E, 1 × 1 m/3 × 3 ft

◆ *Many daphnes are renowned for the scent of their flowers.*

PLANTS *for a* HOT TERRACE

THE HOT TERRACE is ideal, providing the drainage is good, for Mediterranean plants and sun lovers. Plants with leaves that are woolly, waxy, silver or narrow and small tolerate drought most readily, but should never be allowed to dry out.

Cordyline australis **'Atropurpurea'** Slow-growing tender plant. E, 7.5 × 2.4m/25 × 8ft

◆ *This New Zealand cabbage palm bears plumes of fragrant flowers when 8–10 years old.*

Helianthemum (Rock rose)
Makes mounds of evergreen
foliage topped with bright
flowers.
E, 15 × 60cm/6in × 2ft

Dianthus **'Waithman's
Beauty'** A neat, ground-
hugging pink, appreciating
good drainage and lime in
the soil. E, 10 × 15cm/
4 × 6in

Convolvulus cneorum
Glistening silver-green
leaves, flowering all
summer. Not fully hardy.
E, 60 × 60cm/2 × 2ft

**Mesembryanthemum
(Livingstone daisy)**
Succulent leaves. Bright
flowers open in sun.
15 × 15cm/6 × 6in

COLOUR IS VERY MUCH A MATTER OF
INDIVIDUAL TASTE, but, if you fancy a
change from red and shocking pink,
this beautiful cistus illustrated
opposite in dazzling white with the
blue of the ceanothus, set off by the
silver and grey foliage plants,
produces a bright but cooler effect.

Ceanothus impressus A vigorous evergreen shrub with deep
green glossy leaves and many clusters of flowers in early
spring. Californian 'lilacs' are not the hardiest of shrubs,
but grow so well on a wall that they are worth risking.
E, 3 × 3m/10 × 10ft

Lavandula (**Lavender**) An indispensable fragrant shrub that
is the source of lavender oil. There are many types, some
with white or pink flowers, others with leaves that vary from
apple green to silver. Attractive to bees and butterflies. E,
30cm–1.2m/1–4ft height and spread

PLANTS *for a* SHADY TERRACE

IN A SHADY POSITION foliage assumes great importance, as woodland plants tend to be less floriferous and brightly coloured than sun lovers. Plants with large lush leaves that wilt and scorch in sun and wind will thrive in moist shade. Colour is an important consideration. White and gold are the most dramatic colours in shade. Variegated foliage will provide pools of light against green backgrounds.

Hydrangeas are excellent shrubs for mid and late summer in light shade and moisture retentive soils. The dying flower heads turn an attractive colour and should not be pruned away until growth starts in the spring. Flower colour can be affected by the acidity/alkalinity of the soil.

***Aucuba japonica* 'Variegata'**
Few shrubs tolerate shade as
well as aucubas. A
variegated form will
brighten any dark corner.
E, 3 × 2 m/10 × 6 ft

***Camellia* 'Inspiration'**
Camellias thrive best in
light, acid soils. They prefer
dappled shade, or a cool
wall. ◑, E, 3 × 2m/10 × 6ft

***Rhododendron* 'Praecox'** Rosy mauve flowers early in the
year; best protected from frost by overhead tree canopy. All
rhododendrons need acid soil. ◑, E, 1.2–2 × 1.2–2m/
4–6 × 4–6ft

◆ *Winter aconites,* Eranthis hyemalis, *are very effective planted
around rhododendrons.*

Fatsia japonica This is grown for its handsome evergreen foliage and dramatic white flowers in autumn. 3 × 3m/10 × 10ft

Parthenocissus henryana Self-clinging climber. Variegated leaves, best in shade, brilliant red in autumn. 10m/30ft height

Pernettya (Gaultheria) mucronata Lime-hating. Berries in autumn, colour dependent on variety. E, 1.2m × 60cm/4 × 2ft

Convallaria majalis (Lily of the valley) Arching stems carry sweet smelling flowers in early spring. 15 × 60cm/6in × 2ft

Bergenia cordifolia A tough plant with shiny, leathery leaves. Pink early-spring flowers. E, 30 × 60cm/ 1 × 2ft

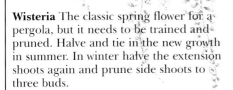

Wisteria The classic spring flower for a pergola, but it needs to be trained and pruned. Halve and tie in the new growth in summer. In winter halve the extension shoots again and prune side shoots to three buds.

PERGOLAS

A PERGOLA ADDS AN EXTRA DIMENSION to your terrace. It provides shade in summer and is a great way to display climbers. To grow well the plants will need to be placed in a border or in 60cm/2ft planting holes. It may help the more delicate climbers to put wires or netting on the posts for extra support. When combining climbers on a pergola, check that pruning regimes are compatible.

2. POTS AND HANGING BASKETS

CHOOSING POTS

CONTAINERS COME in all shapes and sizes. Large pots are easier to maintain as they do not dry out as quickly as small ones. All pots must have drainage holes. Terracotta is the traditional material for ornamental pots, but make sure that your pot will withstand frost if it is left outside in winter.

SITING CONTAINERS

CONTAINERS can enliven dull corners,
fill gaps in borders, hide manhole
covers, distract the eye from ugly
buildings, make herb gardens by the
kitchen door or hold scented plants
near a seat. They are movable gardens
and are also more easily renewed.

Phormium (**New Zealand flax**) and *Aruncus dioicus* This
shows how effective a pot can be when temporarily placed
by a border with the plants complementing each other. The
bronze form of phormium shows up well against the cream
background.

Colour co-ordinated pots. Many different plants grouped together can look something of a hotch-potch but care with the choice of shape and colour makes this an attractive feature.

◆ *Unity is added to the group by using pots of the same material.*

Containers need to be in scale with their surroundings. This large, handsome pot provides the focus of attention for the terraced area. It would be satisfactory, even if not planted.

1. The base of a clay pot will require 'crocking' – pieces of broken pot put in to cover the drainage hole(s) and prevent soil loss. The holes in plastic pots are generally smaller and do not need crocks.

2. Choose a pot larger, but not too much so, than the root ball. Scrape some of the old top layer of compost off the root ball and carefully tease out some roots.

3. Next choose the appropriate compost for your plant, lime-free, or quick-draining, or with added water-retaining granules.

4. Part fill the pot, leaving room for the root ball. Fill round the plant, nearly to the rim, firming carefully.

Plants will suffer in pots if they outgrow them. Replant perennials in fresh compost in a larger container. They can alternatively be divided or you can trim the roots of shrubby forms by about a quarter.

PLANTING *a* CONTAINER

PLANT YOUR BULBS IN AUTUMN for spring flowering. If your winters are very cold, store the containers in a shed or protect with sacking. Many bulbs will rot if frozen solid and the soil in pots is much more vulnerable to freezing than in the open ground.

Spring Pots. The variegated ivy stands out brightly against the hedge, the tulips and primrose adding a welcome splash of colour.

◆ *The effectiveness of the group is increased by the differing heights of the pots.*

PLANTS *for* SUN

ANNUALS AND SOFT PERENNIALS provide
many of the plants suitable for pots on
sunny patios.

Heliotropium × *hybridum*
(**Cherry pie**) Corymbs of
scented flowers all summer.
Not hardy.
30 × 45cm/1 × 1½ft

Agave americana (**Century
plant**) Succulent with sword
leaves, tipped with spines.
Dangerous to children. Not
hardy. 1 × 1m/3 × 3ft

Felicia amelloides (**Blue
marguerite**) Not hardy, so
collect seeds or take
cuttings.
45 × 30cm/1½ × 1ft

Plumbago capensis A
beautiful container shrub,
flowering all summer, but
needs to be frost free.
1.5m × 60cm/5 × 2ft

Containers carefully chosen, grouped together and packed
with plants, make a spectacular display. The colour
of the silver **helichrysum** and pale blue
lobelia complement each other and set
off the shocking pink **pelargonium**.
The blue *Convolvulus sabatius*
shows up well with the
glistening white
marguerite.
Trailing plants
help to bind
the
design
together.

PLANTS *for* PART SHADE

IT IS IMPORTANT to choose plants for
shade that are adapted, like
woodlanders, to live in low-light
conditions. Those preferring sun will
grow lank, with pale leaves and few
flowers, if grown in shade.

There are many varieties of **Hosta**, from large plants,
suitable for a barrel, to plants for a small pot. Silver or gold
variegations look good in the shade.

◆ *Watch out for slugs in the early spring when the leaves are
unfurling.*

Euonymus fortunei Makes an effective standard.
E, 4.5 × 1.5m/15 × 5ft unpruned

◆ *There are many variegated varieties available.*

Pieris japonica Evergreen shrub, with red young shoots and racemes of white flowers in spring. E, 3 × 3m/10 × 10ft

◆ *Pieris needs a lime-free soil and must not dry out.*

Polystichum setiferum 'Acutilobum' (Soft shield fern) The attractive fronds retain their colour all winter. 1 × 1m/3 × 3ft

Lilium regale Beautiful fragrant summer-flowering lily. Stem rooting, so plant deeply. 1.2–2m/4–6ft tall

Cassiope **'Muirhead'** Dwarf heath-like shrub with white bell flowers in spring. For lime-free soil.
E, 10 × 30cm/4 × 12in

Tradescantia virginiana **'Purple Dome'** A hardy plant, flowering from early summer to autumn.
60 × 45cm/2 × 1½ft

Magnificent specimens of *Fuchsia* **'Checkerboard'** and *F.* **'Orange Mirage'** raised on a plinth.

◆ *A high-phosphate feed in summer helps flowering.*

TUBS *and* BARRELS

MOST TUBS AND BARRELS used in the garden are wooden. These should be treated on the inside so that the wood does not rot, either with a preserving fluid or by briefly burning the inside of the barrel to produce a thin protective layer of charcoal.

This copper tub makes a splendid centrepiece to this circle of roof tiles and granite sets.

◆ *The apricot red and yellow shades tone well with the blue-green of the copper.*

***Camellia*
'Anticipation'**
Camellias make
excellent shrubs for
a large container of
the acid, humus-rich
soil they relish. With
the aid of rollers,
the barrel may be
moved from its
prominent
flowering position
and placed so that
it retreats into the
background for
the rest of
the year.

Before filling the trough with compost, cover the drainage holes with crocks.

Top dress the compost with gravel to keep the plants' necks dry to help prevent rotting.

This attractive trough of pansies and lobelia will give a long display if fed and dead-headed.

◆ *In front, both flowers and seed-heads are beautiful.*

SINKS *and* TROUGHS

SINKS AND TROUGHS are most
commonly used for small alpine
plants. Attractive, semi-permanent
miniature gardens can be created in
this way, but narrow troughs can also
be planted like window boxes, the
display changing with the seasons.

The trough shown opposite is used here for a splendid
spring effect. Again the planting has been kept unfussy and
simple, just two: grape hyacinths (muscari) and double
daisies (*Bellis perennis*).

◆ *The spires of the muscari contrast well with the saucer-flowers of
the daisies.*

HYPERTUFA

STONE TROUGHS ARE INCREASINGLY RARE and also expensive. An alternative is to make a hypertufa trough. Hypertufa is a very versatile material and can look good quite quickly.

1. Hypertufa is made from one part each of cement, dry sharp, or concreting, sand and finely sieved peat or coco fibre. PVA bonding agent will give strength and flowability. Mix and add water, mixing until the compound just flows.

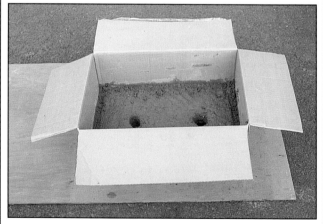

2. Find two boxes to give walls 4–5cm/1½–2in thick. Put the base layer in the larger box and make two drainage holes. Tamp. Place the second box centrally on the base. Larger troughs need wire reinforcement for the base and sides.

3. Support the sides of the outer box and fill the inner box with sand, then continue filling the sides. Tamp. Cover with wet fabric and leave for 36 hours. Carefully remove fabric and boxes.

4. Shape with old knives and a stiff brush. Open up drain holes. Replace wet fabric and leave to set for 2 or 3 days, when it will be strong enough to move. Plant one week later.

SAFETY

Take care not to get concrete products into your eyes and on the skin. Wear goggles and gloves. Wash well when the job is complete.

These chimney pots make an interesting group with the wall pots. They also look good with hanging plants.

A large glazed jar with its agave, and the trellis work, gives an exotic air to a patio.

These alpines and dwarf conifers are growing very happily in this old iron bath and make a very satisfying group with the iron pot spilling its red rock rose onto the gravel.

◆ *The imaginative placing of the iron pot distinguishes this grouping.*

UNUSUAL CONTAINERS

A PLANT-CONTAINER CAN BE ANYTHING that holds compost from a plastic ice-cream tub to a lead cistern. All that is required is some growing medium and drainage holes. Pots can be painted, or clad in wood for effect.

This barrow, with its load of startling white marguerites (argyranthemums), dangling pink pelargoniums and blue lobelia, is cleverly placed in front of a yew hedge which provides an ideal background.

HANGING BASKETS

HANGING BASKETS PROVIDE additional space for plants, add height to your displays and can be placed at different levels to enliven a boring wall. They can be hung on any strong structure to make a display in the middle of your patio.

The bright colours in these baskets are beautifully set off by the grey stone wall.

Hanging baskets are ideal for
trailing plants, like **ivy-leaved
pelargoniums** and **lobelia**
which form great cascades,
while **petunias** and **impatiens**
(busy lizzies) add bulk. These
will make a colourful display all
summer if well fed, watered
and dead-headed.

PLANTING *a* BASKET

CHOOSE AS LARGE A BASKET as the
situation allows; larger baskets dry out
less quickly than smaller ones. A liner
is required to hold in the planting
compost and moisture. There are
various types available, including the
traditional sphagnum moss, but here
we show how to plant up a basket
using a simple polythene liner.

1. The aim is to plant the basket sufficiently densely that the liner is not visible, just a complete sphere of flowers. Before filling the basket with soil, cut holes in the liner around the sides.
2. Gradually fill the basket with planting compost, moisture granules and fertilizer (if this is not already present in the compost), putting plants through the holes you have made as the basket fills up.

3. Cut off any spare liner. Squeeze in a good number of plants to produce a well covered basket and then water thoroughly. It will take three or four weeks for the plants to develop sufficiently to cover the basket. During this time it may be best to keep the basket in an easily accessible, sheltered place for watering before hanging it in its final location.

This combination of perlargoniums (geraniums), petunias, calceolarias and impatiens (busy lizzies) makes a colourful display.

Diascia vigilis This hardy diascia will grow happily in a hanging basket and, with a little trimming, will look good all summer.

Lotus berthelotii This spectacular silver-leaved plant enjoys sun and adds drama to any hanging basket.

Blue lobelia is a very useful foil to reds and pinks, cooling strident shades. Easily raised from seed.

Plants *for* Baskets

Plants for hanging baskets need to be tough to survive in their exposed environment. Trailing plants and those which produce a mass of blooms on short stems to cover the basket with foliage and flowers are a better choice than those with tall rigid stems.

A much rounder effect is gained by using only one type of plant. In a mild winter, these pansies will flower until spring.

◆ *Even in winter, water will be required, especially in cold windy weather.*

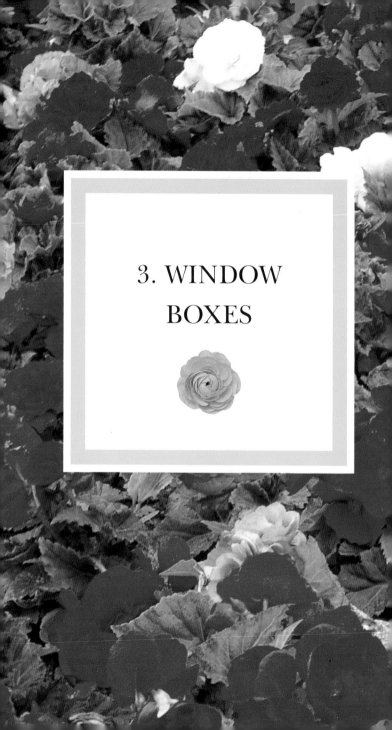

3. WINDOW

BOXES

WINDOW BOX SYSTEMS

TRY TO CHOOSE A SIMPLE WINDOW BOX in style with your building – a hay rack may look out of place on a modern block, or too ornate a box may dominate your plants. Above all, whatever you choose must be secure and able to bear the weight of soil and plants.

A simple restraining bar can be very effective, allowing the use of plants in pots which can be changed through the seasons to maintain the display.

◆ *Take care that top-heavy plants cannot fall over the bar.*

A SPRING DISPLAY

WINTER DISPLAYS OF PANSIES and
evergreens can easily be changed to
spring displays with the help of
daffodils, tulips or hyacinths to give
extra colour and stronger shapes and
to contrast with the existing plants.

This combination of clipped boxes, ivies and skimmias will
have provided interest all winter and the scented flowers of
the skimmias now herald spring.

These rich violet pansies and glowing yellow tulips would
brighten any dull spring day.

◆ *Fewer colours often make a greater impact.*

SUMMER BLOOMS

NOW IS THE TIME FOR EXTRAVAGANT GROWTH and vibrant colours. A little planning will give a dramatic display which, with a little maintenance (feeding, dead-heading and watering), will last well into autumn.

The shocking pink petunias, red ivy-leaved pelargoniums (geraniums) combined with the dashing orange shades of the nemesia and cooled by the dark blue white-eyed lobelia, make a stunning display.

◆ *The white walls and curtains make a perfect cool background.*

Petunia These are well suited to a sunny position but are less happy in a rainy season. A mainstay of most window boxes.

The petunias, verbena and pelargoniums, plants with similar requirements, combine very well to give a good display.

Gazania Sun-loving cream and yellow flowers well set off by bright silver foliage.

The white fuchsia and the apricot and yellow marguerites are highlighted by the bright blue lobelia.

A display of trailing pelargoniums giving continuous colour and good, disease-resistant foliage.

Impatiens (busy lizzies) have a tidy habit, flower continuously and are happy in shade.

Tuberous begonias are available in many colours and, with their shining foliage, give a tropical air.

Zonal pelargoniums are strongly growing, upright plants and can make a fine display on their own.

The pendulous begonias add a luxuriant feel with their shiny pointed leaves and lush satiny flowers glowing against the blue-mauve of the zonal pelargonium.

AUTUMN *and* WINTER

UNLESS YOU LIVE IN A FROST-FREE ZONE,
most of your summer and autumn
plants will be dead by mid-winter, but
there are many hardy evergreens
which will brighten this season.

The griselinia adds height
and substance to this
arrangement.

◆ *These shrubs can be kept for
several winters.*

This is an effective
arrangement of silver and
gold foliage with the splash
of red berries.

◆ *An occasional trim will keep
the little shrubs smart.*

This combination of evergreens
makes a satisfying display. The
heathers will flower in late winter and
set off the clipped **boxes** which give
shape and height. The **ivies** trail,
softening the edges and countering
the rigid shapes of the boxes and
heathers.

INDEX OF PLANTS